ANIMAL ARCHITECTS

How **BIRDS**
Build Their Amazing Homes

W. Wright Robinson

BLACKBIRCH PRESS, INC.
WOODBRIDGE, CONNECTICUT

Acknowledgement
The author thanks Dr. Robert Ake for his help
in reviewing all or part of the material for this book.

Dedication
To my lovely, curious wife, Sharifeh, whose excitement for life
touches all who know her.

Published by Blackbirch Press, Inc.
260 Amity Road
Woodbridge, CT 06525

©1999 by Blackbirch Press, Inc.
First Edition

e-mail: staff@blackbirch.com
Web site: www.blackbirch.com

Printed in Hong Kong

10 9 8 7 6 5 4 3 2 1

Library of Congress Cataloging-in-Publication Data
Robinson, W. Wright.
How birds build their amazing homes / W. Wright Robinson.
    p.   cm. — (Animal architects.)
   Includes bibliographical references and index.
   Summary: Describes the different designs and construction techniques used by various
birds to build nests that best suit their needs. Also provides information about particular
species mentioned.
   ISBN 1-56711-376-1 (library binding : alk. paper)
   1. Birds—Nests—Design and construction Juvenile literature. [1. Birds—Nests.]
I. Title. II. Series.
QL675.R 586 1999   99-26008
598.156'4—dc21   CIP
                                                      AC

Contents

Introduction 4

1 Why Birds Build Nests . . .6
Many Types of Nests 7

2 Sewn Nests 12
Needle and Thread 13
Adding the Lining 14

3 Floating Nests 16
Hidden and Safe 18
Going Down! 19

4 Mound Nests 20
Building the Mound 21
Too Hot or Too Cold? 23
A Full-Time Job 25

5 A Ton of Nest 27
Eagle Aeries 28
Recycling the Nest 31

6 Edible Nests 32
Unusual Building Material . .33
Extra Work 35

7 Clay Nests 37
Mixing and Molding 38
Secret Room 38
Out of the Oven 41

8 Hanging Nests 42
Weaving the Grasses 43
Keep Out! 45
Feet as Nests 45

9 Tunnel Nests 48
Miners at Work 49
High and Dry 51

10 Haystack Nests 52
Building the Roof 53
Bird Motel 54
Long-Term Housing 56

Classification of Birds 57
Common Names and
Scientific Names 59
Glossary 60
Source Notes 61
For More Information 62
Index 63

Introduction

The dictionary describes an architect as "a person whose profession is to design buildings and direct their construction." But people are not the only architects in the world! Human architects are at the end of a long line of remarkable builders. We are actually the most recent builders on the planet. Millions of years before the first human built the first building, animals were building their homes. Some even built large "cities."

Animal architects do not build from drawings or blueprints. Rather, they build from plans that exist only in their brains. Their building plans have been passed from parent to offspring over the course of millions of years.

Meet the Animal Architects

This book will introduce you to just a few of the many fascinating animal architects in the world today. You will discover how they design both resting and living spaces, cradles in which to raise their young, and places to gather and store their food. Most important, you will see how their buildings help them survive in the natural world.

Each group of animals has its own unique methods of construction. Clams, snails, and a few of their relatives build some of the most beautiful structures in all of nature. Their empty homes are the seashells you find at the beach.

Bees, ants, termites, and wasps are among the most interesting architects in the world of insects. They work alone or in large groups to build some remarkably complex homes. Some nests grow larger than a grocery bag and can include five or six stories, with entrances and exits throughout.

Spiders are magnificent architects whose small, often hard-to-find silk homes are every inch as complex and amazing as the larger homes of birds and mammals. Some spiders actually build trapdoors to hide themselves and ambush prey. Others construct beautiful square silken boxes as traps, while they hang suspended in the air!

Birds are another group of remarkable architects. Most people think a bird's nest is simply made of sticks and grass in the shape of a bowl. While this shape describes some nests, it by no means describes them all. Some, like the edible saliva nests of the swiftlets, for example, are quite unusual. In fact, our human ancestors may have learned to weave, sew, and make clay pots from watching winged architects build their nests!

The constructions of mammals are some of the grandest on Earth. Mammals are thinking animals. They can learn from their experiences and mistakes. Each time one of these animals builds a new home, it may be constructed a little differently, a little faster, and a little better.

I hope that you will enjoy reading these books. I also hope that, from them, you will learn to appreciate and respect the incredible builders of the animal world—they are the architects from whom we have learned a great deal about design and construction. They are also the architects who will continue to inspire and enlighten countless generations still to come.

W. Wright Robinson

Why Birds Build Nests

The nests that birds build are among some of the most awe-inspiring structures in the natural world. What's more, birds' nests come in an amazing variety of sizes and shapes. Only a few kinds of birds live in their nests year-round. For most birds, the nest is used only to start and raise a family; it is not their home. When young birds are ready to leave the nest, their parents usually leave, too.

The nests that birds build serve two important purposes. First, a nest is a cradle for the birds' eggs. An egg must be kept safe and constantly warm so a baby bird, or chick, can develop inside it.

Second, a nest is a nursery for young chicks after they hatch. The parents must then feed their young and protect them from harm until they can take care of themselves. Baby birds face many dangers—especially the weather. High winds can blow eggs or young birds out of a nest, or they could be smashed by hailstones in a storm. During summer or winter, the extreme temperatures can destroy the eggs. There are also many animals that like to eat eggs, chicks, and even adult birds. Because of these threats, some birds have found fascinating ways to make their nests safe while they give their eggs and young the care and protection they need.

Many Types of Nests

When most people think of a bird's nest, they think of sticks and grass formed into the shape of a bowl, resting in the branches of a tree. While this description fits some nests, it does not fit them all.

The variety of bird nests is amazing. Some birds build nests above ground, but others build them on or below the ground. There are some nests that float in ponds and marshes, and some that hang down and swing from branches. Some are made of rocks—and some are actually the bird's own feet! There are even nests that people eat or wear. Some birds sew and some birds weave. A few birds use mud to hold their nests together. Others glue their nests in place.

There are almost as many different kinds of nests as there are different kinds of birds.

Clockwise from top left: cliff swallow, young crested cormorants, pileated woodpecker with young, blackeyed bulbul.

Clockwise from top: blue jays, American redstarts, herring gull with eggs, tree swallow.

As you can see from the table on pages 10-11, the same family of birds may build two or three different types of nests. For example, there are many different types of penguins, and each builds a different nest. The type of nest some birds build depends on where they live and what materials are available for them to use. For example, an albatross may simply scrape a spot on the ground and lay its eggs there if no building materials are in the area. When sticks are nearby, these same birds may use them. If the proper building materials are available, an albatross may build a more typical cup-shaped nest.

You will also find that not all birds build nests. Some birds simply do without them altogether. A good example of this is the emperor penguin. The tops of its feet are all it ever needs to make a "nest" for its young.

NEST DESIGNS OF THE WINGED ARCHITECTS

Stick nests:

Albatross
Avocet
Antpipit
Cassowary
Cormorant
Crane
Duck
Finfoot
Frigatebird
Grouse
Guineafowl
Gull
Hawk
Hemipode-quail
Heron
Ibis
Kagu
Lark
Limpkin
Loon
Osprey
Owl (typical)
Painted snipe
Parrot
Pelican
Phalarope
Pheasant
Pigeon
Rail
Screamer
Seedsnipe
Tinamou
Whale-billed stork

Rock nests:

Penguin

Mud nests:

Babbler
Flamingo

Nests with no structure:

Auk
Barn owl
Gull
Nightjar
Penguin
Potoo
Pratincole
Sandpiper
Shearwater
Thick-knee
Tropicbird

Nests in a ground scrape:

Albatross
Avocet
Booby
Bustard
Collared-hemipod
Emu
Loon
Ostrich
Oystercatcher
Phalarope
Plover
Pratincole
Rhea
Sandgrouse
Seedsnipe
Skimmer
Skua
Thick-knee
Tinamou
Turkey

Feet nests:

Penguin

Mound nests:

Megapode
Pratincole

Floating nests:

Coot
Grebe
Gull
Jacana
Loon
Rail

Cup-shaped nests:

Albatross
American wood
 warbler
Antbird
Babbler
Bulbul
Finch
Flamingo
Grouse
Mockingbird
Oilbird
Old World flycatcher
Pheasant
Pipit
Sparrow
Starling
Thrush
Troupial
Tyrant flycatcher

Roofed nests:

American wood
 warbler
Antbird
Babbler
Dipper
Lark
Lyrebird
Ovenbird
Pitta
Rail
Wren

American vulture
Auk
Barbet
Barn owl
Bee-eater
Crab plover
Crow
Diving-petrals
Duck
Gull
Kiwi
Motmot

New Zealand wren
Ovenbird
Owl (typical)
Penguin
Puffbird
Puffin
Rail
Sandpiper
Shearwater
Sheathbird
Storm-petrals
Swallow tanager
Tapaculo
Titmouse
Tody
Tropicbird
Tyrant flycatcher

BIRDS THAT BUILD NESTS ABOVE THE GROUND

Open stick nests:

Anhinga
Antpipit
Boat-billed heron
Booby
Cormorant
Creeper
Crow
Cuckoo
Curassow
Duck
Falcon
Finfoot
Frigatebird
Frogmouth
Gull

Hawk
Heron
Hoatzin
Honey-eater
Hoopoe
Ibis
Limpkin
Mesite
Osprey
Pelican
Pigeon
Plantcutter
Rail
Secretary bird
Shrike
Silky flycatcher
Stork
Sunbittern
Touraco
Vangashrike

Hanging nests:

Antbird
Asity
Broadbill
Bulbul
Drongo
Flowerpecker
Honey-eater
Manakin
Oriole
Pepper-shrike
Sunbird
Titmouse
Troupial
Tyrant flycatcher
Vireo
White-eye

Mud nests:

Cotinga
Mudnest-builder
Swallow

Saliva nests:

Crested swift
Hummingbird
Swift

Hole nests:

American vulture
American wood
   warbler
Antbird
Barbet
Barn owl
Bird of paradise
Cotinga
Crow
Cuckoo-roller
Falcon
Finch
Hoopoe
Hornbill
Jacamar
Kingfisher
Motmot
New Zealand wren
Nuthatch
Old World flycatcher
Ovenbird
Owl (typical)
Owlet-frogmouth
Parrot
Pigeon
Pipit
Roller
Starling

Swallow
Swallow tanager
Swift
Tanager
Tapaculo
Thrush
Titmouse
Toucan
Trogon
Trumpeter
Tyrant flycatcher
Weaverbird
Woodhoopoe
Woodpecker
Wood-swallow
Wren
Wryneck

Nests on a bare tree limb:

Fairy tern

Roofed nests:

American wood
   warbler
Babbler
Cuckoo
Dipper
Hammerhead stork
Honey-eater
Lyrebird
Old World warbler
Ovenbird
Pitta
Tanager
Tapaculo
Titmouse
Tyrant flycatcher
Wren

Sewn Nests

Most people think of a tailor as a person who makes clothes out of fabric and sews with a needle and thread. But not all tailors are human. There are also tailors in the world of birds. Tailorbirds are smaller than sparrows. These little birds do, in fact, sew their nests together and they actually do use a kind of "needle and thread." They are found mostly throughout Asia, China, and India.

Needle and Thread

When it is time to build a nest, a tailorbird searches for a large leaf hanging on a tree. While the leaf is still attached to the branch, the bird punches a few holes along both outside edges of the leaf, using its long, pointed beak like a needle.

Before it can begin sewing, a tailorbird must find some "thread." Sometimes, the bird uses the silky strands from a spider's web or stringy fibers from a plant. Tailorbirds living near humans may find a real piece of string or thread to use. Once it has found the thread, the bird pulls on the leaf with its feet and beak until the two punched edges of the leaf overlap. The tailor then carefully pushes the thread through the holes with its beak and pulls the thread tight. To keep the thread from coming out of the holes, this clever, creative bird sometimes ties a knot in one end of it. It then punches more holes along the sides of the leaf and continues stitching. Soon, the bird has made a sturdy cone-shaped leaf container.

SEWING SMALL LEAVES

If a tailorbird cannot find a large enough leaf for its nest, the little builder will stitch two leaves together. It will punch holes along both edges of the two leaves. Then, it will join the two leaves by stitching them together along the edges to make its nest.

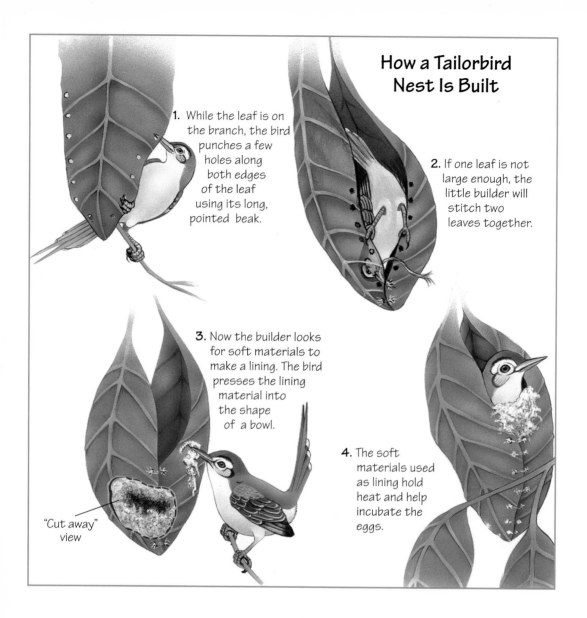

How a Tailorbird Nest Is Built

1. While the leaf is on the branch, the bird punches a few holes along both edges of the leaf using its long, pointed beak.

2. If one leaf is not large enough, the little builder will stitch two leaves together.

3. Now the builder looks for soft materials to make a lining. The bird presses the lining material into the shape of a bowl.

"Cut away" view

4. The soft materials used as lining hold heat and help incubate the eggs.

Adding the Lining

Now, the bird looks for soft materials to make a lining for its leafy home. It may find sheep's wool or some other soft fur that an animal has shed. If the bird cannot find enough material to line its nest, it may also add soft plants. After a tailorbird has put the fiber lining inside the nest, it presses the lining into the shape of a small bowl. This bowl becomes a safe, sturdy nest in which the bird lays its eggs and raises its young. Before the eggs hatch, the parents must sit on them to keep them warm. The soft hairs and plant fibers within the nest help hold this warmth around the eggs and help to incubate them.

A tailorbird's nest is very safe. Because the leaf that was used is still alive and hanging on the tree, the nest is well camouflaged, or disguised. It blends in perfectly with its natural surroundings. It is not easy for enemies to see the nest, so the eggs and young chicks remain hidden and are kept safe from danger.

Feathered Facts: Tailorbirds

Common names:	Tailorbird or long-tailed tailorbird
Scientific name:	*Orthotomus sutorius*
Family:	Old World warbler (Sylviidae)
Range:	India, Sri Lanka, southern China, Malaysia, and Java in Indonesia
Kind of nest:	Leaf nest made by sewing one or two leaves into a pouch, then lining the nest with hair or soft plant matter.
Number and color of eggs:	About three eggs, pinkish or bluish-white, with a few reddish-brown spots
Parents' tasks:	Male and female birds may share nest building and egg incubation or female may do it herself.

Floating Nests

Many birds live and make their nests near water, but only a few actually make their nests *on* the water. The phrase "floating nests" may make you think of ships in a bird navy. A floating nest isn't exactly a ship, but it is a clever way to raise a family in a place that's safer than most. Floating nests are built by birds called grebes.

Male and female grebes work together to collect marsh reeds and shoreline grasses for their floating nest.

Building a nest on water may seem like a difficult task, but these nests are actually very simple to construct. Working together, the male and female grebe collect marsh reeds and shoreline grasses that grow around the nest site. They carry the plants in their mouths to the edge of a lake or pond and pile them on the water. The female grebe then lays her eggs on top of this floating, grassy pile.

The tall marsh grasses that often surround a grebe nest anchor it and hide it from possible enemies.

Hidden and Safe

Often, floating nests are found in marshes among tall grasses growing at the water's edge. Marsh grasses hide the nest and anchor it in one place so that it will not float into open, dangerous areas. Because the nest is hidden, the eggs and young are protected from animals that may try to harm them.

Sometimes, however, nests do drift out of the marsh grasses and float into the open water. Even then, one of the parents will sit on top of the nest, keeping the eggs warm while bobbing around on the lake or pond.

Going Down!

As time passes, the raft-like nest becomes waterlogged. The grasses, soaked with water, begin to sink very slowly. By the time the chicks hatch, their raft is damp and soggy.

Chicks that are raised on these soggy floating rafts, however, get along just fine. Grebes are actually not as helpless as some other baby birds. When they hatch, their eyes are open and they already have soft down feathers to keep them warm. Not long after hatching, they are able to swim around with their parents and, a few days later, can even gather some of their own food.

Feathered Facts: Grebes

Common name:	Pied-billed grebe
Scientific name:	*Podilymbus podiceps*
Family:	Grebe (Podicipedidae)
Range:	Canada, the United States, and some parts of South America
Kind of nest:	Raft nest made of plant parts heaped along the shoreline of a pond or lake.
Number and color of eggs:	Four to seven eggs. Eggs are greenish-white or bluish-white when laid, but are stained to a greenish-brown color by the nest material.
Parents' tasks:	Both male and female build the nest and take turns incubating the eggs.

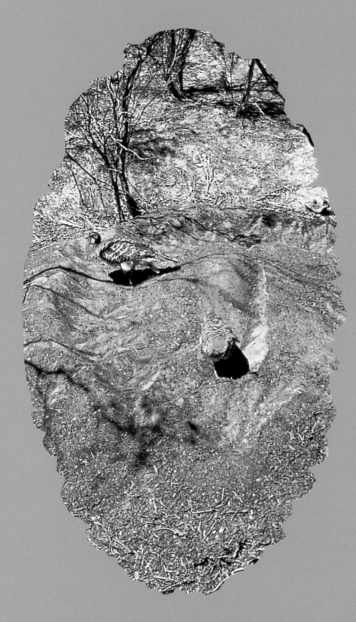

Mound Nests

In and around Australia, there are birds that have a unique way of incubating their eggs. Instead of sitting on their eggs and using their body heat, they bury their eggs in large mounds of sand. These mounds act as giant incubators that keep eggs at a remarkably constant temperature. The birds that build these structures are called mound builders, or incubator birds.

The mound builders actually warm their eggs with the heat that comes from the breakdown of dead plant materials. When a plant dies, it rots and eventually becomes part of the soil again. This rotting is called decomposition, and it is caused by natural bacteria and other factors. As plant matter breaks down, a small amount of heat is created.

One of the most interesting kinds of mound builders is the mallee fowl of central and southern Australia. The male is very hard working and dedicated to hatching the chicks. He spends a total of eleven months each year building and taking care of his mound nest! His mate only helps a little.

Building the Mound

The continent of Australia is south of the equator. Europe and North America are north of the equator. When it is summer in the regions north of the equator, it is winter in the regions south of the equator.

In April or May, which is autumn in Australia, the male begins working on his mound. First, he digs a pit about 3 feet (1 meter) deep and more than 6 feet (2 meters) wide in sandy soil. Then, he fills the pit with dead plants that he finds near-by. Carefully, he covers the rotting vegetation with sand. When he has finished, the mallee fowl has built a mound about 3 feet (1 meter) high and more than 15 feet (5 meters) wide.

Now, the bird must wait for the decomposing plants to raise the temperature deep inside the mound to about 93° F (34° C). This process takes about four months. The male does not stop working, however. While he is waiting, he replaces the sand on the outside of his mound as the wind blows it away. He also checks the temperature inside the mound each day.

A male mallee fowl will work almost constantly throughout the year to maintain his nest and regulate the temperature within it.

Too Hot or Too Cold?

Male and female incubator birds check the temperature inside their mounds by using the very sensitive temperature organs in their beaks. When they hold decomposing plants in their mouths, the temperature organs act as thermometers, indicating if an area inside the mound is too hot or too cold.

By September, the incubator mound is ready for the eggs. The male digs a hole in the mound, and both he and his mate check the temperature in the area around the hole. If both birds are satisfied that the temperature is correct, the female lays an egg in the hole. Her mate then covers the egg with sand.

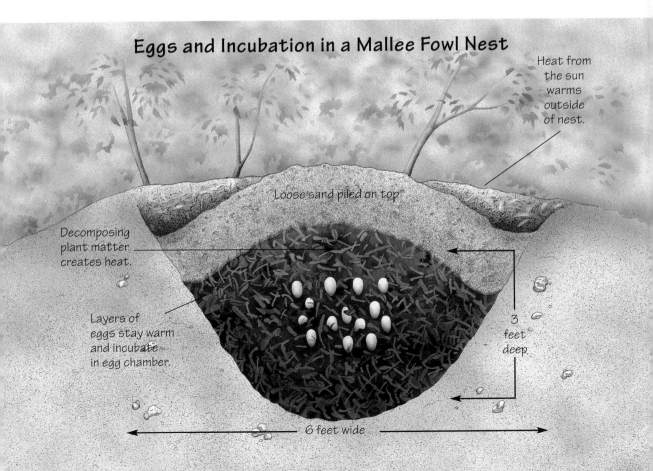

Eggs and Incubation in a Mallee Fowl Nest

Heat from the sun warms outside of nest.

Loose sand piled on top

Decomposing plant matter creates heat.

Layers of eggs stay warm and incubate in egg chamber.

3 feet deep

6 feet wide

Mallee fowl have sensitive organs on their beaks that enable them to keep their nests at a constant temperature.

If, however, one of the birds is not satisfied with the temperature, the female does not lay her egg there. Instead, that hole is covered, and a new one is dug. Every five to ten days, the pair returns to the mound so the hen can lay another egg. During a single breeding season, she may lay thirty to thirty-five eggs in the mound.

For a chick to develop, each egg must incubate for fifty days. Because the female did not lay all her eggs at the same time, all the chicks will not hatch together. It may be seven months from the time the first egg is laid until the last chick is hatched.

A Full-Time Job

The mound must be kept at the same temperature until all the chicks hatch. While the eggs are incubating, the male checks the temperature inside the mound every day. With hard work, he is able to keep the mound within one or two degrees of the desired temperature. His job, however, is not always the same. He must keep the incubator mound at about 93°F (34°C) during three seasons: spring, summer, and autumn. This is not an easy job because the temperature outside the mound can change drastically and can affect the temperature inside the mound.

During September—Australia's spring—the decomposing plants in the mallee fowl's mound are producing plenty of heat—sometimes too much. If the temperature around the eggs becomes too warm, the male digs a hole in the mound to let some of the heat out.

As summer approaches, many of the plants have already decomposed, and the heat within the mound is not as great as it was in the spring. The hot summer sun, however, can easily overheat the eggs, so the male adds more soil to the mound. By making the mound thicker, he prevents the sun's heat from penetrating the mound and harming the eggs.

In autumn, when the sun is weaker, a mallee fowl will expose its eggs during the day, to warm them before covering them up for the night.

When autumn arrives, the plant decomposition is finished, and heat is no longer being produced inside the mound. The sun is cooler and now only warms the soil during the middle of the day. During this time, when the sun is warmest, the male opens the mound and lets in the sun's warmth. While he removes the dirt, he also spreads it around the mound so it can warm in the sun along with the exposed eggs. In late afternoon, he covers the eggs again with soil, which provides warmth through the cool night.

After a chick hatches, it digs its way to the top of the mound to get out. When it finally reaches the surface, the father—who has worked so long and hard for this moment—does not even greet the new chick. In fact, the father and his newborn chicks have nothing to do with one another! They do not even seem to recognize each other and remain strangers for life.

Feathered Facts: Mallee Fowl

Common name:	Mallee fowl
Scientific name:	*Leipoa ocellata*
Family:	Megapode (Megapodiidae)
Range:	Southern and central Australia
Kind of nest:	Mound nest of rotting plants and soil or sand.
Number and color of eggs:	Thirty to thirty-five tan eggs
Parents' tasks:	Male constructs the nest with some help from the female; female lays one egg every five to ten days; male tends nest.

 5

A Ton of Nest

When you look at a huge building, you don't usually think about how much it weighs. Most often, you simply marvel at its sheer size. Well, it's no different with birds' nests. A large nest on the ground—like the mallee fowl's mound nest—is impressive because of its size. But a huge nest like that up in a treetop or perched on a rock ledge is even more amazing because it rests high in the air.

Eagle Aeries

Big, heavy nests built way up high, sometimes called aeries or eyries, differ from most other nests in two important ways. First, the nests are used year after year by the original builders, or by a different pair of birds of the same type.

The second difference is that aeries are built with sticks and small branches instead of twigs and grass. This means that the builders need to be big. Bald eagles, for example, are builders of large stick nests. These huge birds are also very strong fliers, which helps them carry heavy loads of branches up to their "construction sites."

For an architect, the first step in building a structure is finding a good site. The first step in building any nest is the same. Where a nest is built depends on the kind of bird that is building it and the area in which it lives. A pair of bald eagles, for example, usually nests in the top of a very tall tree or on a rocky ledge, high up. After bald eagles choose a nesting site, they begin gathering sticks and branches.

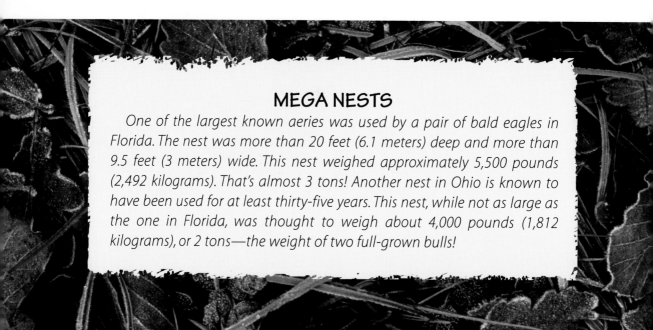

MEGA NESTS

One of the largest known aeries was used by a pair of bald eagles in Florida. The nest was more than 20 feet (6.1 meters) deep and more than 9.5 feet (3 meters) wide. This nest weighed approximately 5,500 pounds (2,492 kilograms). That's almost 3 tons! Another nest in Ohio is known to have been used for at least thirty-five years. This nest, while not as large as the one in Florida, was thought to weigh about 4,000 pounds (1,812 kilograms), or 2 tons—the weight of two full-grown bulls!

Eagle aeries are some of the largest and heaviest bird nests in the world. Built high up in trees or rocky ledges, some nests can weigh 4,000 pounds (1,812 kilograms) or more.

Newborn eagles (eaglets) will remain in the aerie until they can fly.

Some of the sticks may be as long as 6 feet (2 meters). The male and female birds put all the sticks in a pile at the nesting site, eventually building a platform. Next, they add soft grasses and feathers to the center of the platform. This soft area is where the eggs are laid and where the young remain until they can fly.

Recycling the Nest

For most birds, nests are not meant to be homes; they are used only to raise their young. Bald eagles are different, however. They often continue using their nests after the young eagles leave. Before the female lays her eggs the following year, however, the birds add new, clean sticks to the nest.

If the original builders leave the area, another pair of parents may choose to take over the ready-made nest. They, too, will add new sticks to the pile that is already there. As time goes by and new generations use the structure to raise their young, the nest becomes larger and heavier. It is easy to understand why these nests can eventually weigh a ton or more.

Feathered Facts: Bald Eagles

Common name: Bald eagle

Scientific name: *Haliaeetus leucocephalus*

Family: Hawk (Accipitridae)

Range: North America

Kind of nest: Stick nest formed from a pile of large branches with a grass-and-feather lining.

Number and color of eggs: Two or three white eggs

Parents' tasks: Both the male and female build the nest, although the female may do most of the work; female probably incubates the eggs.

Edible Nests

People around the world have very different tastes in food. What one culture considers a "delicacy" may be distasteful to another culture. For more than 200 years, people in China have collected and eaten the nests built by small birds called swiftlets. Today, these edible nests can be bought throughout the world. The builders of the nests, however, live only in Asia.

Unusual Building Material

Swiftlets use saliva to build their nests. Saliva is the liquid that helps to keep an animal's mouth moist, but the saliva used to build these nests is very different. When the swiftlet's saliva dries, it becomes very hard. This is an efficient building material for making a nest. This way, the swiftlets don't have to spend valuable time and energy looking for materials to use. The only thing the birds have to do is find a good site for their nest. They usually choose a place high on the walls of huge caves. By putting their nests in such a location, the swiftlets help shelter themselves and their young from bad weather and, at the same time, keep their homes well out of the reach of animals that may harm their young babies.

BIRD'S NEST SOUP

The nests built by Asian swiftlets are considered a delicacy by many people. How does one eat a bird's nest? One of the most popular ways is in a soup, appropriately called bird's nest soup. In this popular Asian dish, the nests are cooked and seasoned to taste very good. Unfortunately, they are expensive and have very little nutritional value.

Sticky saliva attaches to rocks and other surfaces to create a swiftlet nest.

After a good site is found, the male swiftlet begins building the nest. First, he pushes a drop of his special saliva onto the rock wall with his tongue. The saliva is sticky, and more of it is constantly being released into the swiftlet's mouth. Because of this, as the bird moves his head away from the wall, a thin strand of saliva extends between him and the drop on the wall. The swiftlet moves his head around so that the saliva thread forms a crescent, or half-circle, shape on the rock. Then, the bird adds more saliva to the shape. As layer upon layer of saliva threads build up, the crescent eventually becomes a half-bowl. When it is done, the half-bowl serves perfectly as a nest.

A STICKY SITUATION

Asian swiftlets are not the only birds that use saliva to build their nests—hummingbirds also use this method. They do not, however, make pure saliva nests. Instead, they build their nests of plant materials and use their sticky saliva as glue to hold the materials together. Unlike swiftlet nests, hummingbird nests are not edible.

Hummingbird nests are made of saliva and other natural materials.

Extra Work

The nests that result are almost pure saliva. Unfortunately for the birds, these are the ones most valued by people as food. If a swiftlet's nest is taken by collectors, it must start the building process all over again.

The second nest is not usually made of pure saliva, because the birds only have a limited amount of it. As their supply of saliva is used up, the swiftlets must use other materials to complete their structure. Humans often take this second nest structure from the birds, too, although it is not as valuable.

If the second nest is taken, the swiftlets must build a third structure from pieces of plants glued together with the little saliva that is left. Not particularly valuable, these nests are left by collectors for the birds to use.

Feathered Facts: Swiftlets

Common name:	Swiftlet
Scientific name:	*Collacalia* species
Family:	Swift (Apodidae)
Range:	Asia
Kind of nest:	Bowl-shaped nest constructed of saliva, sometimes with other materials added.
Number and color of eggs:	Two white eggs
Parents' tasks:	Male builds the nest; female lays and incubates eggs.

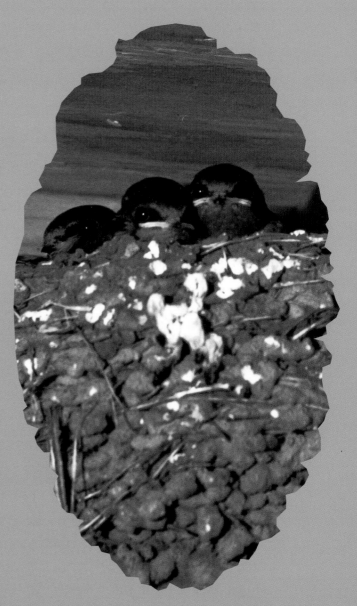

Clay Nests

Potters are people who make pots out of clay. Just as humans find many uses for clay and mud, so do many kinds of birds. One of the most interesting nests made out of clay is the type built by rufous ovenbirds. They were given their name because their nests are hollow balls of hardened clay with an opening in one side, similar to the baking ovens that were used by some Native American Indians and early European settlers.

Rufous ovenbirds are a little larger than sparrows and live mostly in Central and South America. When it is time to build a nest, the male and female work together because there is a great deal to be done. From start to finish, it takes the pair about two weeks to gather materials and build their nest. During this time, they must collect about 2,000 pieces of clay!

Mixing and Molding

Some ovenbirds choose to build their nests on top of a fence post, on the branch of a tree, or on the roof of a house. Once the birds find a good place for their nest, building begins. A male and female first collect bits of clay to construct the floor. They may then mix some grass with the clay. As the clay dries and hardens, the grass holds it together, making the nest stronger. When the grass-clay mixture is ready, the birds use their beaks and feet to put it down just where they want it. They continue until they have a solid floor for their nest.

Next, the ovenbirds build the walls of their clay nest on the sturdy foundation. As the walls get higher, the builders curve them inward and form a dome-shaped roof. They leave a hole in one of the walls to use as a door.

A Secret Room

To complete the nest, the birds build a wall inside the clay ball, dividing the space into two "rooms." The wall reaches from the floor of the nest almost to the roof. The birds leave a small gap at the top so that they can move from one room to the other. Just inside the doorway is a very narrow front room. On the other side of the wall is a large back room, where the eggs are laid. Grasses and other soft materials line the floor there.

How an Ovenbird Nest Is Built

1. A male and female collect mud and mix it with grass to begin building the "floor" of their nest in the bough of a tree.

2. The pair builds sides that curve to form a roof. They build an interior room with a small entrance. They leave an opening in one side for an exterior door.

1.

2.

3.

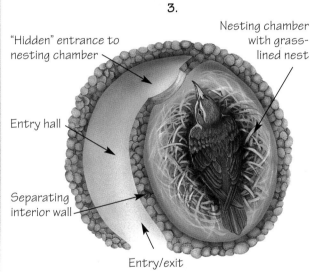

"Hidden" entrance to nesting chamber

Nesting chamber with grass-lined nest

Entry hall

Separating interior wall

Entry/exit

Why do ovenbirds build a nest with two rooms if they only use one? It may seem like extra work, but it does have a purpose. If the ovenbirds built a one-room house and a predator looked inside, it would find the eggs or young birds and eat them. To keep this from happening, the ovenbird puts up a wall between the nest's door and the area where the eggs lie. If an animal looks inside, it sees nothing but an empty room. This way, the occupants of the nest are kept safely out of sight.

Ovenbird nests are covered nests made mostly from mud. They average about 1 foot (30 centimeters) wide and often weigh about 10 pounds (4.5 kilograms).

Out of the Oven

After about two weeks of work, the finished nest, about 1 foot (30 centimeters) across and weighing almost 10 pounds (4.5 kilograms), is used for only a short time. Like most other birds, ovenbirds use their nests only for raising young—not as a home. The period from the time the eggs are laid until the young birds fly away is only about six weeks.

Like most birds, ovenbirds use their nests only for hatching and raising their young.

Even if they wanted to, ovenbirds couldn't stay in this nest much longer than six weeks. As summer approaches and the hot sun beats down on the clay, the temperature inside rises. Now the nest really does become an oven! Inside, the birds would not be able to survive the heat.

Feathered Facts: Rufous Ovenbirds

Common name:	Rufous ovenbird
Scientific name:	*Furnarius rufus*
Family:	Ovenbird (Furnariidae)
Range:	South America
Kind of nest:	Clay and grass dome with two interior "rooms."
Number and color of eggs:	Three or four white eggs
Parents' tasks:	Both male and female build the nest and incubate the eggs.

Hanging Nests

Can you imagine a person wearing birds' nests as shoes? Children in eastern Europe sometimes wear the warm, sturdy nests of one type of little bird as slippers in winter! This "shoemaker" bird, known as the penduline titmouse, is smaller than a sparrow. In some parts of eastern Africa, members of at least one tribe are known to use this kind of bird's well-woven nest as a purse.

Weaving the Grasses

In early spring, a male titmouse begins making a nest. Working alone, he must first find a long, strong piece of grass. Carrying the grass in his beak, he flies to the end of a tree branch and circles it many times, twisting and turning. Eventually, one end of the grass strip becomes securely fastened to the branch; the other end hangs free beneath it. The bird then attaches more strips of grass in the same way.

Once this master builder has attached many grass strips to the branch, he separates them into two groups. He takes a piece of grass from each group and, using his beak and feet, weaves the two ends together. After he has woven all the hanging strips, the nest looks like a basket with a handle.

The nest now has two walls and a floor. The next step is to build the back wall. To do this, the penduline titmouse weaves more grass between the handles and the bottom of the basket. When this work is finished, the nest is shaped like a pear with an open front.

This basket-like nest would suit most birds, but it doesn't satisfy the penduline titmouse. This talented architect also adds a front wall to his nest. He leaves a small hole near the top of the front wall to use as a door.

Even though a male titmouse has worked for about a month, and is still not finished, he can at least go out and find a mate. Together, the pair works to complete the nest. They collect parts of plants, like seed fluff, and push them into the outside walls of the tightly woven nest. This fluffy material helps make the nest stronger by making its walls much thicker.

Making a Titmouse Nest

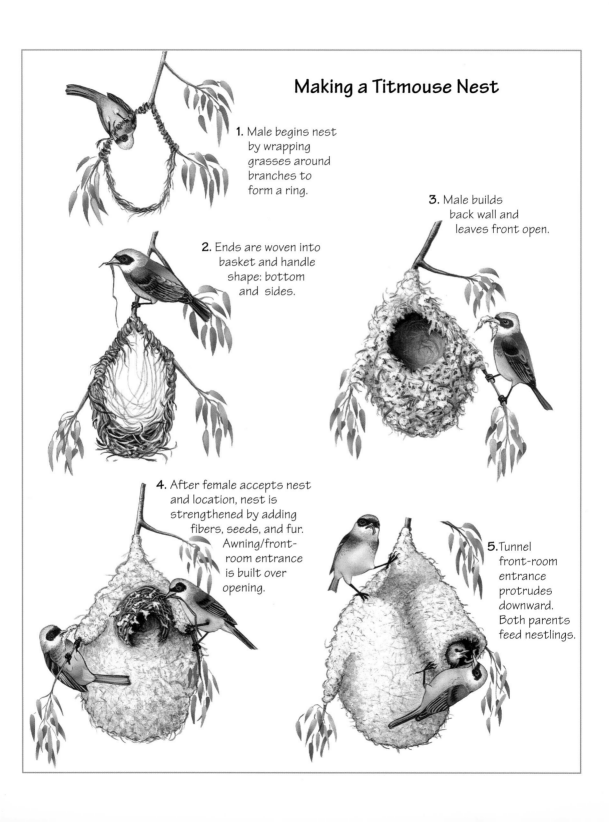

1. Male begins nest by wrapping grasses around branches to form a ring.

2. Ends are woven into basket and handle shape: bottom and sides.

3. Male builds back wall and leaves front open.

4. After female accepts nest and location, nest is strengthened by adding fibers, seeds, and fur. Awning/front-room entrance is built over opening.

5. Tunnel front-room entrance protrudes downward. Both parents feed nestlings.

Keep Out!

Finally, the penduline titmice have finished their woven construction, and the nest is ready to use. This masterpiece is one of the best-built homes in the world of birds. The parents have a very sturdy, warm, dry nest in which to lay their eggs and raise their family. In addition, because the nest hangs at the end of a tree branch where few animals can go, the titmouse family is also safe from enemies.

Some titmice make their nests even safer by building them at the ends of willow-tree branches. These branches are very long and thin and hang straight down, so few animals can climb to the ends of them.

Feathered Facts: Penduline Titmice

Common name:	Penduline titmouse
Scientific name:	Remiz pendulinus
Family:	Titmouse (Remizidae)
Range:	Europe and Africa
Kind of nest:	Tightly woven, pear-shaped nest made of grass and soft plant materials.
Number and color of eggs:	Five to ten white eggs
Parents' tasks:	Male weaves the nest; male and female line the nest; female incubates the eggs.

FEET NESTS

There is probably no place in the world where weather conditions make it more difficult for birds to thrive than near the South Pole in Antarctica. Compared to this area, the freezer section in a grocery store seems warm! Icy blizzards with winds of more than 100 miles (160 kilometers) per hour often last for days. Temperatures sometimes drop below -90° F (-68° C)—that's more than 80°F (26℃) colder than most freezers. Despite the harsh temperatures, emperor penguins thrive in Antarctica.

Emperor penguins are the largest of all penguins. When fully grown, they are about 4 feet (1.2 meters) tall and may weigh more than 75 pounds (34 kilograms). Much of their weight comes from a thick layer of fat, called blubber, that helps keep them warm. Emperor penguins eat fish and other sea life found in the icy ocean waters. To help them swim, their stiff wings work like flippers. Penguin feet are webbed and serve as rudders, helping to steer as they swim.

Penguin chicks stay warm in the "feet nests" of their parents.

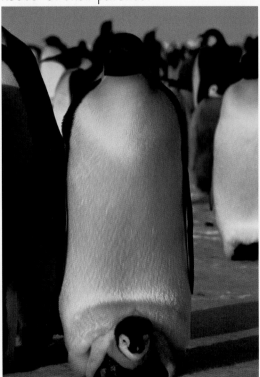

When it is time for emperor penguins to raise their families, they gather on ice near the ocean. This becomes their breeding ground, called a rookery. At the start of the Antarctic winter, during which time the sun never rises, the female lays one pale green egg. With his beak, the male rolls the egg onto the top of his feet to keep it warm. But this alone will not keep the egg warm enough. The top of the egg must also be covered by a loose flap of skin and feathers from the penguin's abdomen. This flap hangs down over the father's feet,

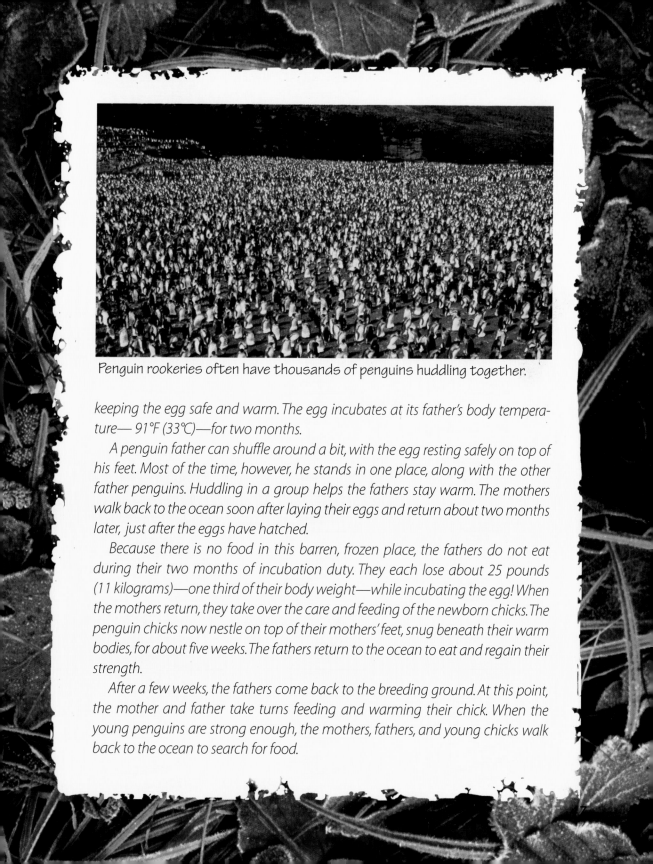

Penguin rookeries often have thousands of penguins huddling together.

keeping the egg safe and warm. The egg incubates at its father's body temperature— 91°F (33°C)—for two months.

A penguin father can shuffle around a bit, with the egg resting safely on top of his feet. Most of the time, however, he stands in one place, along with the other father penguins. Huddling in a group helps the fathers stay warm. The mothers walk back to the ocean soon after laying their eggs and return about two months later, just after the eggs have hatched.

Because there is no food in this barren, frozen place, the fathers do not eat during their two months of incubation duty. They each lose about 25 pounds (11 kilograms)—one third of their body weight—while incubating the egg! When the mothers return, they take over the care and feeding of the newborn chicks. The penguin chicks now nestle on top of their mothers' feet, snug beneath their warm bodies, for about five weeks. The fathers return to the ocean to eat and regain their strength.

After a few weeks, the fathers come back to the breeding ground. At this point, the mother and father take turns feeding and warming their chick. When the young penguins are strong enough, the mothers, fathers, and young chicks walk back to the ocean to search for food.

Tunnel Nests

Not all birds build their nests on the ground or in high places. Some birds make their nests underground. Some of them may simply use an animal burrow that they have found. Those lucky birds have very little work to do. Other birds dig their own underground homes. These "miners" work very hard, and both the male and female share in doing the work of construction.

Building nests in the ground is not as simple as it may seem, because not all soil is safe for tunnels. If the birds do not build in the right kind of soil, the tunnels may collapse and the birds would be buried alive. Generally, tunneling birds look for soil that has some clay in it. Clay is sticky, firm, and is good material for building tunnels.

Miners at Work

A bird that digs its own nest works with its beak and feet. With only these tools, they often dig a long, narrow tunnel deep into the earth, with a slightly larger chamber at its end. This chamber is the actual nest, where eggs are laid and young are raised.

A belted kingfisher enters its burrow-like nest underground.

Kingfishers may work for weeks digging out tunnels and chambers in their burrows.

You may think that a nest located at the end of a tunnel would be very safe. It is—but birds like the belted kingfisher take no chances. Kingfishers add a few extras to make their nests even safer for their eggs and young chicks. A pair of belted kingfishers usually digs their tunnel in the side of a steep bank, high above land or water. Once they decide where the nest should be, the birds take turns flying up to the wall of dirt and pecking at the same spot with their beaks. Each time they peck, a little dirt is knocked loose.

Eventually, the pair chips a small hole into the bank. Now, their work can go faster. They grip the edge of the hole with their tiny feet and loosen more soil with their beaks. As the tunnel in the bank grows deeper, one bird digs while the other kicks the soil out with its feet. A pair of kingfishers may work for 3 weeks to build their tunnel, which can be as much as 10 feet (3 meters) long.

High and Dry

The kingfishers' hard work makes a safe nest for their young. Not many enemies—not even snakes—can climb straight up the steep bank to get into the tunnel. To make life in the nest more secure, the kingfishers also slant the tunnel upward slightly as they dig. This way, if a hard rain beats against the entrance hole, the water won't flow down into the chamber and drown the baby birds.

When the young kingfishers must leave the safety of their nest, they walk to the open end of the tunnel. Suddenly, it's time to fly. The young birds can make no mistakes because the long fall from their high tunnel could kill them. For most young kingfishers, however, that first step out of the tunnel is no problem and they fly away. One day, they may even return to start a family of their own in a nearby steep clay bank.

Feathered Facts: Belted Kingfishers

Common name: Belted kingfisher

Scientific name: *Megaceryle alcyon*

Family: Kingfishers (Alcedinidae)

Range: North America

Kind of nest: Tunnel into the side of a steep cliff or bank, with a nest chamber at the far end of the tunnel.

Number and color of eggs: Six to eight white eggs

Parents' tasks: Both male and female dig out the nest and incubate the eggs.

Haystack Nests

Sociable weavers are birds that live on the African grasslands. These creatures, which are related to sparrows, build huge nests that many birds can live in together. Their nests have often been described as looking like "haystacks in trees." The fact is, however, that these nests are not at all loosely thrown together. They are actually very well built and will often last for many years.

Building the Roof

To begin building their nest, a group of male sociable weavers works together to construct a large roof. Despite their name, these birds do not actually weave. Instead, they push grass, straw, and twigs under the rough bark of a tree branch. When each piece is firmly in place, the little builders find more grass or twigs and wedge them under the bark, too. As many birds pack more and more straw and twigs together, they soon create a very sturdy roof. This roof is similar to the thatched roofs found on some African huts.

Despite their name, sociable weavers do not weave, but they do push grass, straw, and twigs together into a tightly constructed roofed nest.

Bird Motel

Once the roof is ready, pairs of weavers (a male and a female) begin building their own compartments, or nests, beneath it. First, a pair chooses a spot for their nest. Then, they tightly pack together the roof straw and twigs around their site. The birds then build a floor and sturdy walls for their nest by wedging more straw and grass around the site. If the builders choose straw or grass strands that are too long, they simply bite them off to make them fit. The unused pieces fall to the ground and may be used later. The weavers build an entrance hole through the floor on one side of the nest chamber.

When completed, the nest is a globe-shaped compartment about 6 inches (15 centimeters) in diameter. Sometimes, the entire inner chamber is lined with soft plant parts. The builders also add a special feature to their ball-like nest. They build a ledge across the front edge of the entrance hole to keep the eggs from rolling out onto the ground.

Soon, more and more pairs of birds build their nests under the large roof. The sociable weavers' nest is like a motel with many rooms under one roof. All of the doors of the weavers' nests open toward the ground. This type of door makes the nest safer. Most animals, unless they can fly, are unable to reach the eggs, young birds, or parents in the nest. For the weavers, it is just as easy to enter their nests by flying under the roof as it is to fly in from the side.

Each year, other pairs of weavers that join the community add on to the roof. As these birds add new nests, the "bird motel" gets very large. The roofs of some of these nests can become more than 15 feet (5 meters) wide and can house more

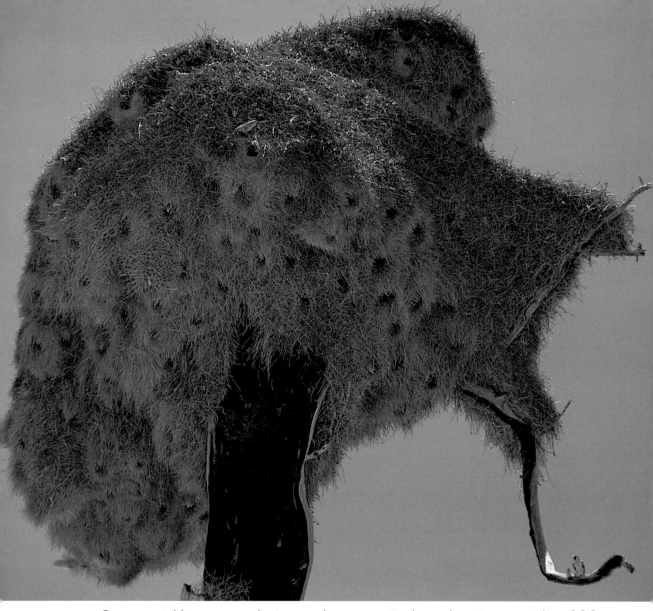

Some sociable weaver colonies can become quite large, housing more than 200 birds at a time.

than 100 pairs of birds, with each pair living in its own individual nest! The thick "thatched" roof protects the eggs and young birds from the hot tropical sun. Even when rainfall is heavy, the birds and their families will remain dry beneath their thick, well-built roof.

Long-Term Housing

After their young fly away to build nests of their own, the parents continue to live in their snug community. There, they can stay protected from the rain and hot sun, and from most dangerous animals.

Some of these large communities have lasted fifty years or more. When birds that live there die, others move into their empty nests. As the years pass, the roof gets larger and larger as the number of occupants increases. Eventually, the huge haystack-like nest becomes too heavy for the tree to support it. The branch snaps, and the nest falls to the ground. At this point, the nest becomes unusable and the weavers that survive must move on to build another community in another tree.

Feathered Facts: Sociable Weavers

Common name:	Sociable weaver
Scientific name:	*Philetairus socius*
Family:	Weaverbird (Ploceidae)
Range:	Southern and southwestern Africa
Kind of nest:	Many nest compartments with downward-opening entrances, built beneath a roof of grass and twigs.
Number and color of eggs:	May be white, reddish, or pale blue or green, with or without spots
Parents' tasks:	Males do most of the roof building; males and females together construct their individual nests.

Classification Chart of Birds

Within the animal kingdom, all animals with similar characteristics are separated into groups. A major group is called a phylum. Similar animals within a phylum are separated into a smaller group called a subphylum. Animals within a subphylum that are most similar to one another are then separated into several smaller groups: class, order, family, genus, and species.

The following table provides information about the phylum, subphylum, class, order, and family of the birds discussed in this book.

Classification	Family	Examples	Number of Species
KINGDOM: Animalia		all animals	More than 1,500,000
PHYLUM: Chordata			
SUBPHYLUM: Vertebrata			
CLASS: Aves (birds)			
ORDER: Sphenisciformes	Spheniscidae	penguin	17
ORDER: Podicipediformes	Podicipedidae	grebe	20
ORDER: Galliformes	Megapodiidae	megapods	12
ORDER: Passeriformes	Furnariidae	ovenbird	215
	Paridae	titmouse	65
	Ploceidae	weaverbird	313
	Sylviidae	Old World warbler	398
ORDER: Coraciiformes	Meropidae	kingfisher	24
ORDER: Falconiformes	Accipitridae	hawk and eagle	205
ORDER: Apodiformes	Apodidae	swift	76

Common Names and Scientific Names

All plants and animals have formal Latin names. Many also have common names, or nicknames. The formal name of a plant or animal is called the scientific name, and it is the same all over the world. A common name, however, can be different from place to place and in different languages.

Common names can sometimes be confusing because different kinds of plants or different kinds of animals may have the same common name. For example, if someone told you that they saw a trap-door spider, you could not be certain whether it was the spider that builds simple tube-like homes, the one that builds wishbone-shaped burrows, or the one that builds burrows with side doors.

In the table below, you will find the common name (nickname) and the scientific name (formal name) for each bird discussed in this book. Each scientific name has two parts.

The first part, called the genus, always begins with a capital letter. The genus includes the small group of animals that are similar to one another in many ways.

The second part of the scientific name, called the species, is not capitalized. The species includes animals that are exactly alike. If the exact species is not known, then the genus name is given alone.

Common Name	Scientific Name
BIRDS	**BIRDS**
Tailorbird or long-tailed tailorbird	*Orthotomus sutorius*
Emperor penguin	*Aptenodytes fosteri*
Pied-billed grebe	*Podilymbus podiceps*
Mallee fowl	*Leipoa ocellata*
Bald eagle	*Haliaeetus leucocephalus*
Swiftlet	*Collacalia species*
Rufous ovenbird	*Furnarius rufus*
Penduline titmouse	*Remiz pendulinus*
Belted kingfisher	*Megaceryle alcyon*
Sociable weaver	*Philetairus socius*

Glossary

aerie (AIR-ee) A nest high above the ground; often refers to the nests of eagles. Also known as an eyrie.

bacteria (bak-TEER-ee-uh) Microscopic plants, some of which are helpful and some harmful. Bacteria are very important in the decomposition of plants and animals.

blubber A thick layer of fat under the skin of sea mammals and penguins that helps keep them warm.

burrow A hole in the ground where an animal lives, hides, and raises its young.

camouflage (KAM-uh-flahzh) A disguise meant to hide something.

chamber An enclosed space, such as a cave, room, or cell.

compartment A separate section or part. A room could be considered a compartment of a house.

decomposition (DEE-kahm-poh-ZIH-shun) A rotting or breaking down of something into its basic parts.

diameter (dy-AM-uh-tur) The length of a straight line that passes through the center of a circle or round object.

down A young bird's first feathers.

eyrie (AIR-ee) Another spelling of aerie.

incubate (IN-kyuh-bayt) To keep in a proper environment for development. Most birds incubate their eggs by sitting on them, keeping the eggs safe and warm.

nursery A place where young are raised.

ornithology (or-nuh-THAHL-uh-gee) The study of birds.

penduline (PEN-dyoo-lihn) Related to the word pendulum, this word describes nests that hang down and swing freely.

phylum (FY-luhm)(plural: fy-la) A large group of plants or animals; one of the primary divisions of the plant and animal kingdoms.

rookery (ROOK-er-ee) A place where many birds of the same kind gather to lay their eggs.

rufous (ROO-fus) Having a rusty or brownish red color.

saliva (suh-LIE-vuh) A liquid produced in the mouth that helps in swallowing and digesting food.

scientific name The two-part Latin name given to every different kind, or species, of organism. Every species has its own scientific name; in this way, an organism that has more than one common name can be properly identified worldwide.

site A place where something is, was, or will be.

sociable Liking to be with others.

social Describes animals that live in an organized group.

species (SPEE-seez) A single category of organism with common characteristics.

waterlogged Soaked or filled with water so that floating is difficult.

wedge To force something into a narrow space.

Source Notes

Dossenbach, H. D. *The Family Life of Birds.* New York: McGraw-Hill, 1971.

Gillard, E. T. *Living Birds of the World.* New York: Doubleday, 1967.

Gooders, J. Birds: *An illustrated survey of the bird families of the world.* London: Hamlyn, 1975.

Harrison, Hal H. *A Field Guide to Birds' Nests (found east of Mississippi River).* Boston: Houghton Mifflin, 1975.

———. *Field Guide to the Birds of North America.* Washington, D.C.: National Geographic Book Service, 1983.

———. *The Wonder of Birds.* Washington, D.C.: National Geographic Book Service, 1983.

Hudson, Robert. *Nature's Nursery: Baby Birds.* New York: The John Day Company, 1971.

Peterson, R. T. *The Birds.* New York: Time, 1963.

Pettingill, O. S. *Ornithology in Laboratory and Field.* Minneapolis: Burgess Publishing, 1970.

Vevers, Gwunne. *Birds and Their Nests.* New York: McGraw-Hill, 1973.

Welty, J. C. *The Life of Birds.* 2nd ed. Philadelphia: W. B. Saunders, 1975.

For More Information

Books

Bennett, Paul. *Making a Nest* (Nature Secrets). Chatham, NJ: Raintree/Steck Vaughn, 1997.

Doris, Ellen. Len Rubenstein (Photographer). *Ornithology* (Real Kids Real Science Books). New York, NY: Thames & Hudson, 1994.

Ganeri, Anita. Danny Flynn (Illustrator). *Birds* (Nature Detective). Danbury, CT: Franklin Watts, Inc., 1992.

Nolting, Karen Stray. Jonathan P. Latimer. Roger Tory Peterson (Illustrator). *Birds of Prey* (Peterson Field Guides for Young Naturalists). Boston, MA: Houghton Mifflin Co., 1999.

Stevens, Ann Shepard. Jennifer Dewey (Illustrator). *Strange Nests.* Danbury, CT: Millbrook Press, 1998.

Web Sites

All About Birds

Learn migration patterns, behavior, and field marks for many types of birds—**www.enchantedlearning.com/subjects/birds/Birdwatching.html**

The Aviary

A great deal of information about bird behavior and anatomy, including a section just for kids—**theaviary.com/bi.html**

Index

Aeries, 27–31
  largest, 28
Albatross, 9
American redstart, 9
Antarctica, 46, 47
Asian swiftlet, 32–34
  facts about, 35

Bald eagle, 28–31
  aerie, 27–31
  eaglets, 30
  eggs, 30
  facts about, 31
  habitat, 31
Belted kingfisher,
  48–51
  chicks, 51
  enemies, 51
  facts about, 51
  habitat, 51
  nest, 49, 51
  tunnel, 49, 50
Bird's nest soup, 33
Blue jay, 9
Bulbul, 8

Camouflage, 15
Caves, 33
Classification, 57
Cliff swallow, 8
Common name, 58

Crested cormorant, 8

Decomposition, 21

Emperor penguin, 46,
  47
  blubber, 46
  chicks, 47
  eggs, 46, 47
  size, 46
Equator, 21
Eyries. See Aeries.

Feet nests, 46–47

Grebe, 16 –19
  chicks, 19
  eggs, 17
  facts about, 19
  habitat, 19
  nest, 17–19

Herring gull, 9
Hummingbird nests,
  35

Incubation, 15, 20
Incubator bird. See
  mallee fowl.

Mallee fowl, 20–26

chicks, 21, 24, 26
eggs, 20, 21, 23–26
facts about, 26
habitat, 26
incubation, 20
mound, 21, 23–26
temperature organ,
  23
Marshland, 17

Native American
  Indians, 37
Nests
  See also individual
    species.
  clay, 37–41
  designs, 10-11
  edible, 32–36
  floating, 16–19
  hanging, 42–45
  haystack, 52–56
  mound, 20–26
  sewn, 12–15
  tunnel, 48–52
  variety, 7, 9

Penduline titmouse,
  42–45
  enemies, 45
  facts about, 45
  habitat, 45

nest, 43–45
Penguins, 46–47
Pileated woodpecker, 8

Rookery, 46–47
Rufous ovenbird,
    37–41
  chicks, 41
  eggs, 41
  facts about, 4
  front room, 38, 39
  habitat, 45

nest, 38–41

Saliva, 33-36
Scientific name, 58
Sociable weaver,
    52–56
  eggs, 55
  facts about, 56
  habitat, 56
  nest, 54
  roof, 53, 55
South Pole, 46, 47

Swiftlet, 32–36
  habitat, 36
  human contact, 33,
    36
  nest, 33-36

Tailorbird, 12–15
  eggs, 15
  facts about, 15
  habitat, 15
  nest, 13–15
Tree swallow, 9

Photo Credits
Cover and title page: ©Corel Corporation; pages 4, 5, 58: ©PhotoDisc; pages 6, 8, 9, 12, 16, 17, 27, 35, 37, 41, 46-48, 52: ©Corel Corporation; page 18: ©Victoria McCormick/Animals Animals; page 20: ©Des & Jen Bartlett/OSF/Animals Animals; pages 22, 24, 25: ©Hans & Judy Beste/Animals Animals; pages 29, 40: ©Fritz Polking/Peter Arnold; page 30: ©Don Enger/Animals Animals; page 32: John A. Novack/ Animals Animals; page 33: ©Mickey Gibson/Animals Animals; page 34: Patti Murray/Animals Animals; page 42: Malcolm S. Kirk/Peter Arnold; page 49: ©John Gerlach/Animals Animals; page 50: ©Marty Stouffer Productions/Animals Animals;page 53: ©Ana Laura Gonzalez/Animals Animals; page 55: ©Michael Fogden/Animals Animals.

Illustration Credits
Pages 14, 23, 39, 44: ©Trudy L. Calvert/TLC Creations.